To the explorers of imagination,

May this book guide you through the centuries, unveiling wonders that transcend time.

May each colored page be a portal to a past rich in stories and extraordinary achievements.

May the beauty of these seven treasures of the world inspire your creativity and transport you to a universe where wonders intertwine with the magic of colors.

With gratitude for the shared journey,

Gigi Garcia

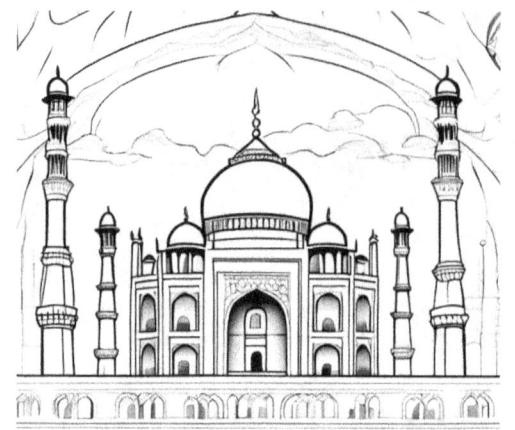
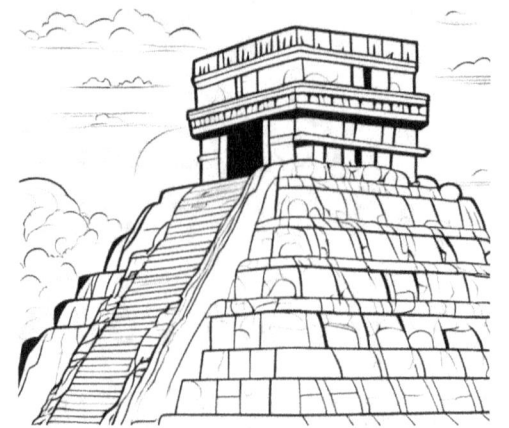

Colors of Wonder: A Coloring Journey Through the Modern Wonders of the World

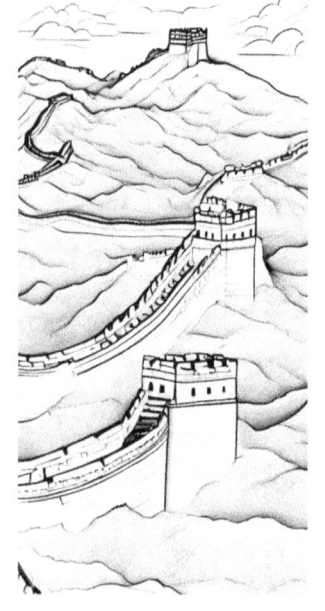
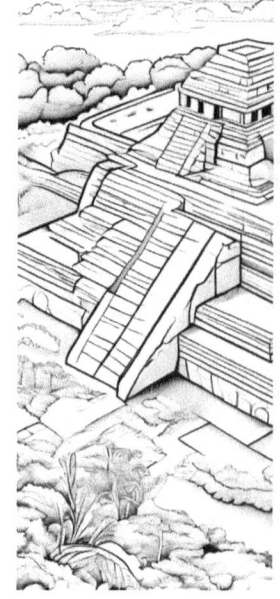

This beautiful book belongs to

_____

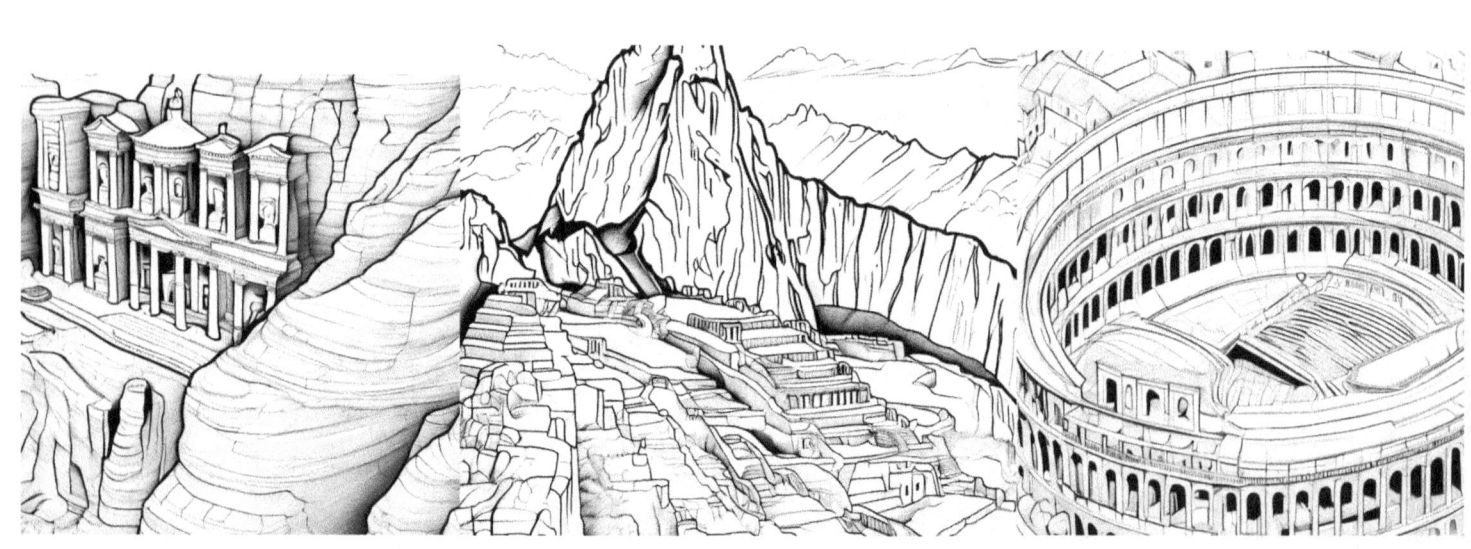

Test Color Page

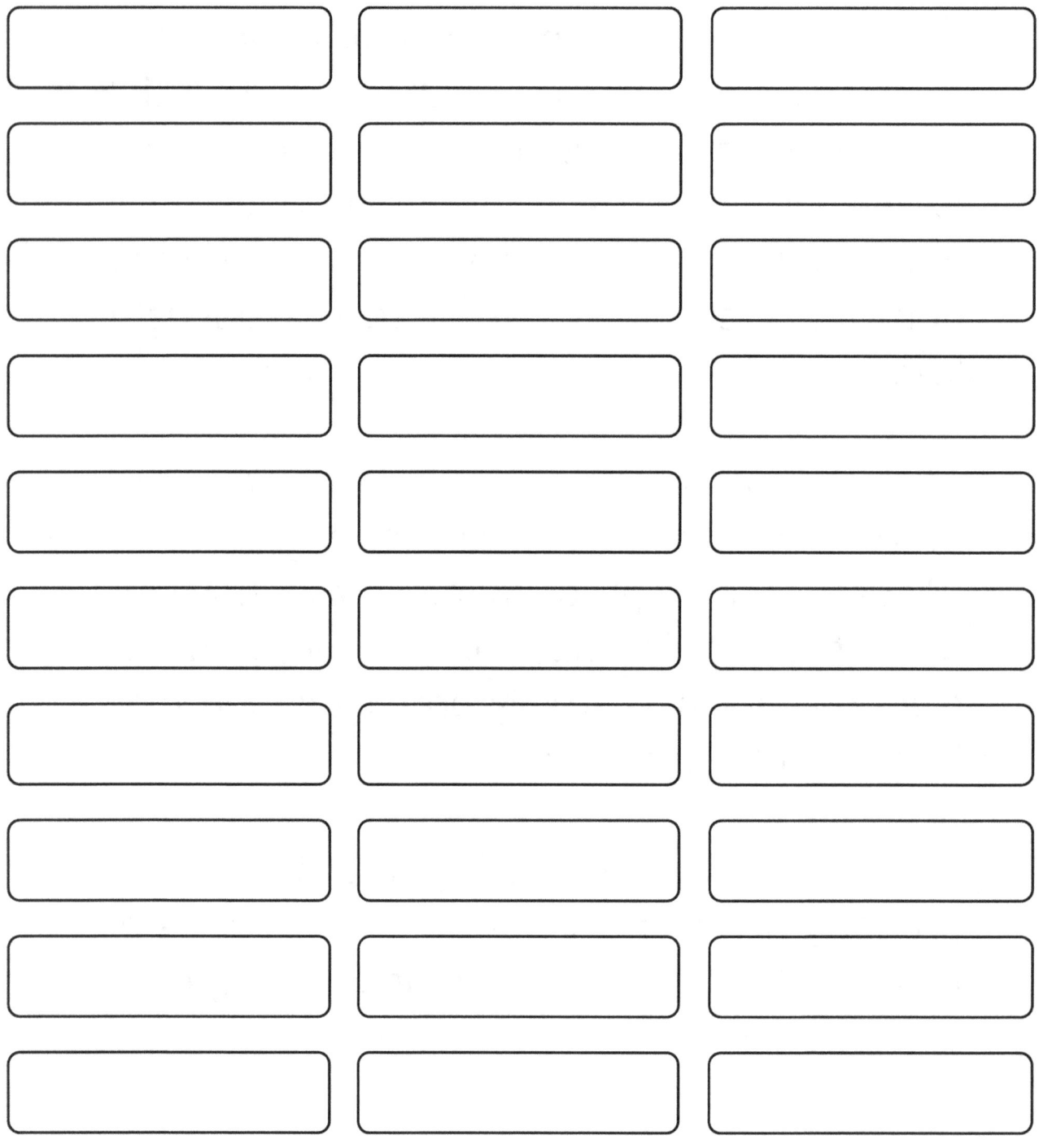

Colors of Wonder: A Coloring Journey Through the Modern Wonders of the World

Welcome to "Colors of Wonder," where art and history converge in a delightful exploration of the Seven Modern Wonders of the World. This coloring book invites you on a vibrant journey through architectural marvels that have left an indelible mark on our global heritage. As you traverse these pages, you become both an artist and an explorer, bringing to life the Great Wall of China, Petra, Christ the Redeemer, Machu Picchu, Chichen Itza, the Roman Colosseum, and the Taj Mahal.

Immerse yourself in the intricate details of each wonder, discovering their stories and significance. Whether you're an avid colorist, a history enthusiast, or someone seeking a creative escape, "Colors of Wonder" is your canvas for a unique artistic adventure. Let your imagination flow and your colors breathe life into these iconic structures. May this coloring journey be a source of inspiration, relaxation, and a celebration of the wonders that captivate our collective imagination.

Happy coloring!

Great Wall of China: A Super Long Wall to Keep China Safe

Built over several dynasties starting in the 7th century BC, the Great Wall of China served as a massive defense against invaders.

Emperor Qin Shi Huang began its construction, connecting the existing walls to create a formidable and very long barrier – more than 21,000 kilometers!

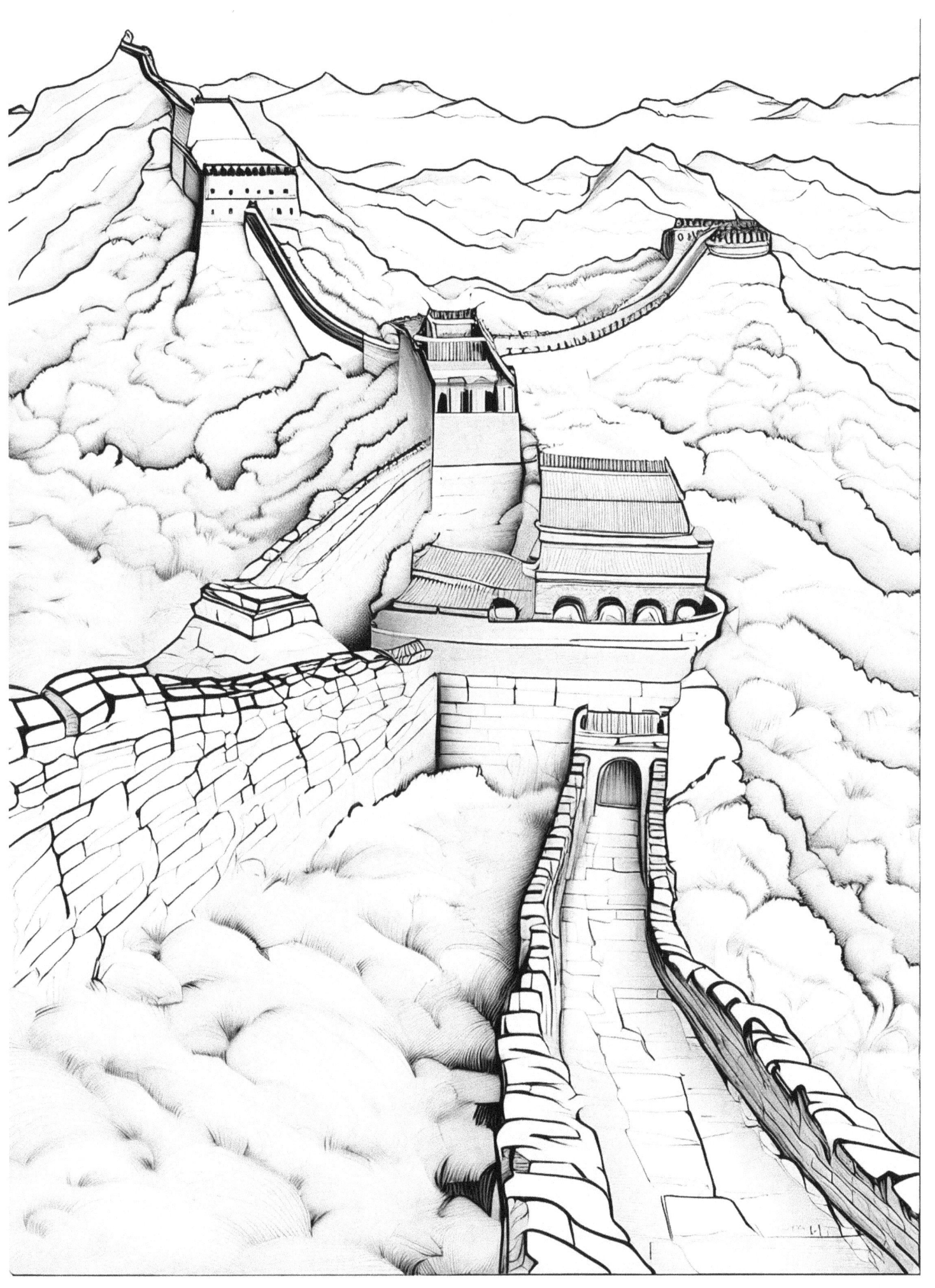

Imagine a huge wall made of stones and bricks winding through mountains and deserts. Along the wall, there are tall towers where people could see if anyone was coming to attack.

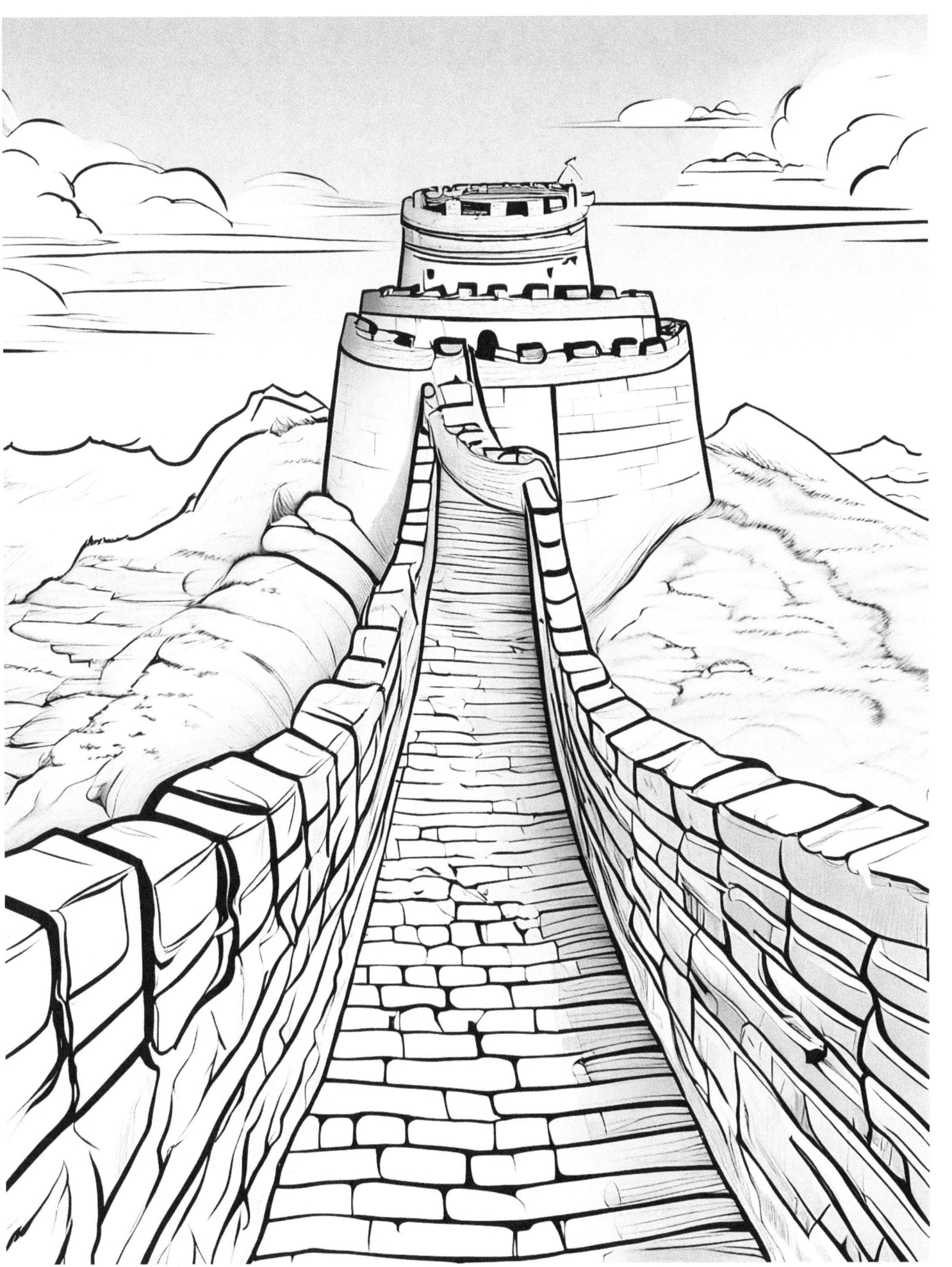

The Great Wall is not just a wall; it is like a long history book that tells how China defended itself and remained strong.

Fun fact: Contrary to popular belief, it is not visible from space without help.

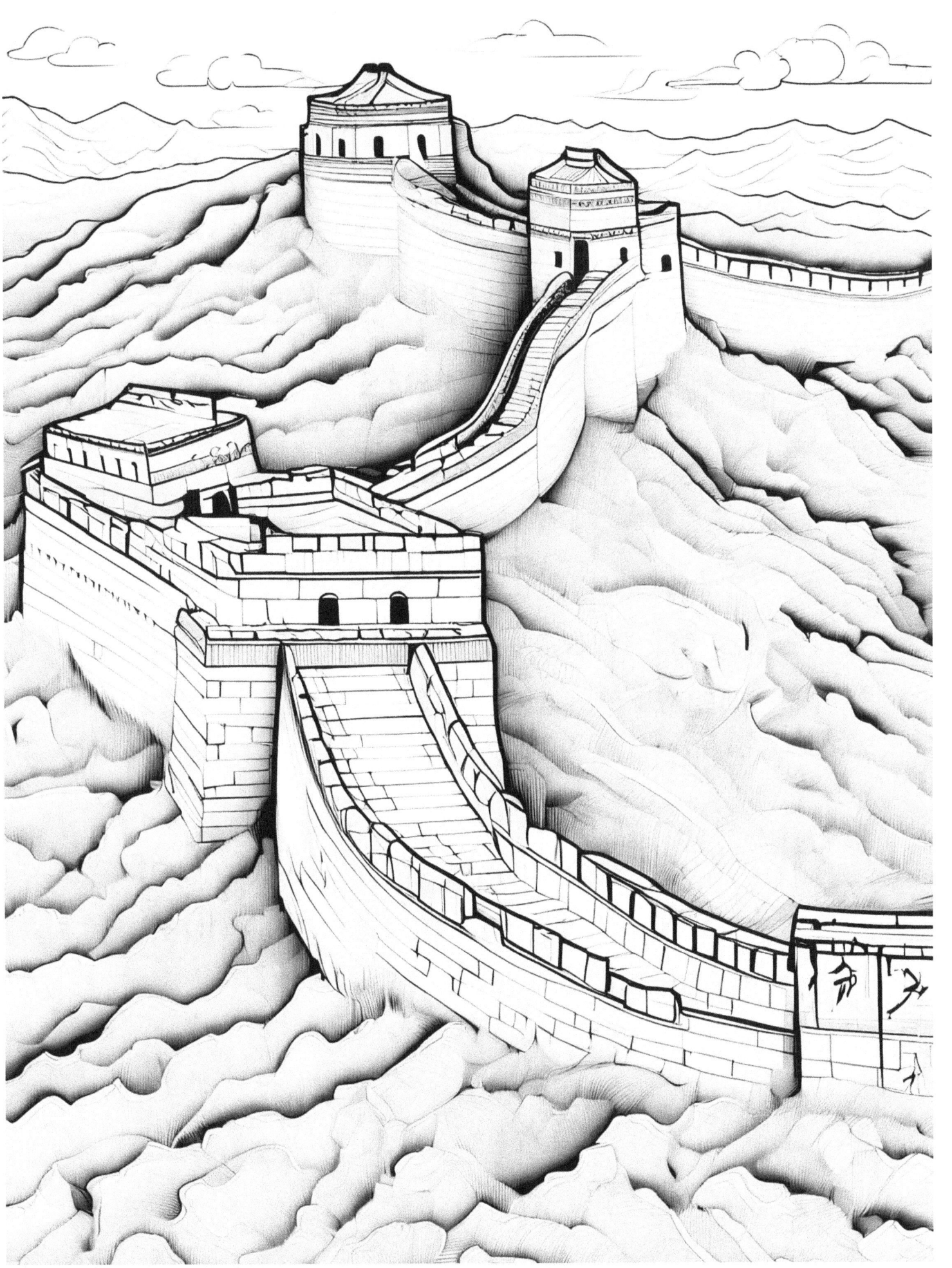

Petra, Jordan: A City Carved in Rocks and Secrets

In Jordan, there's an ancient city called Petra, and what makes it special is that it's carved into rocks.

Imagine buildings made out of big rocks, creating a city hidden in the cliffs.

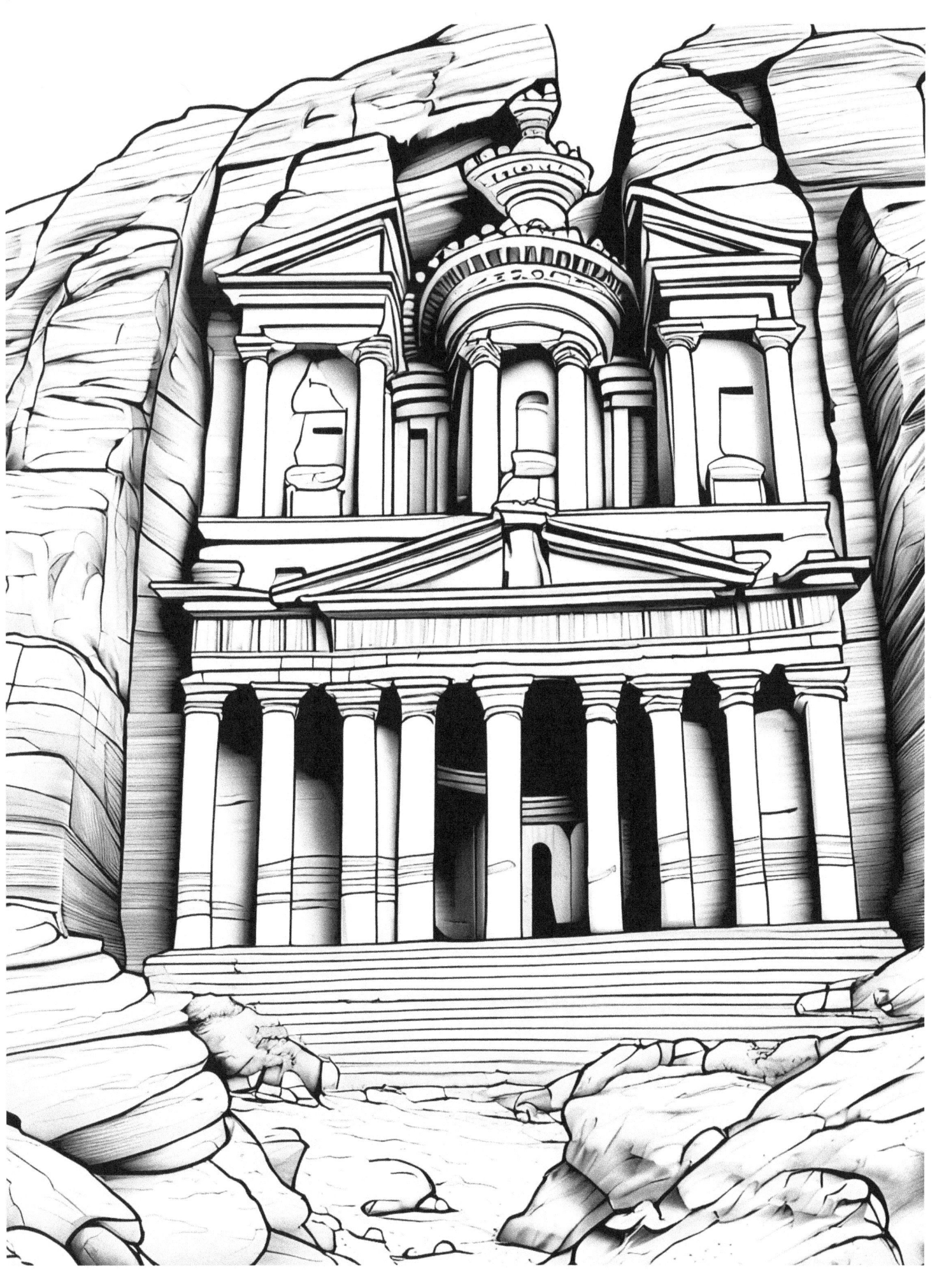

They call it the "Rose-Red City" because of the color of the rocks. People used to live here, and they traded goods.

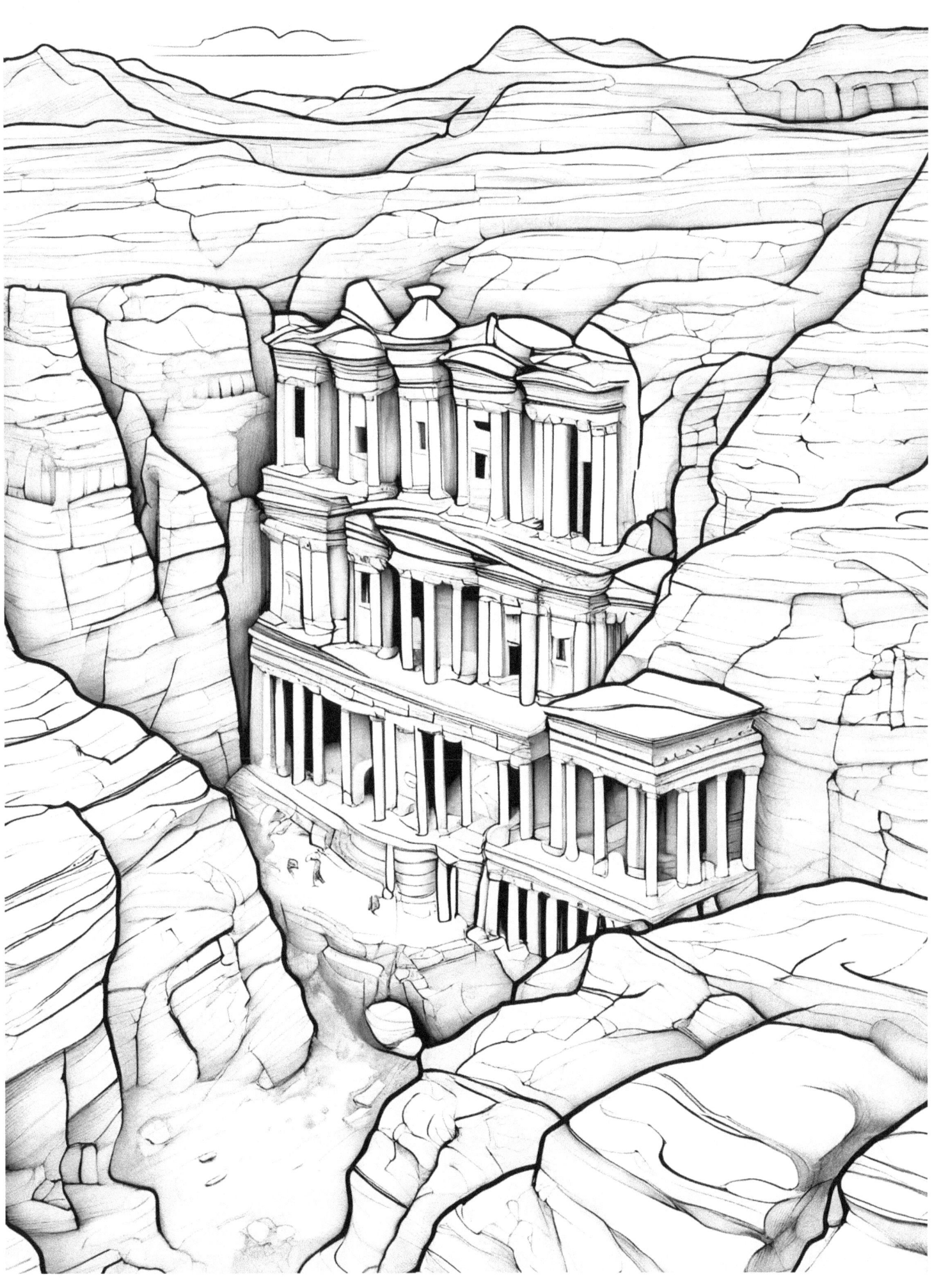

Walking through Petra is like stepping into a time machine, exploring the secrets of an old city tucked away in the rocks.

Curiosity: Petra's intricate rock-cut architecture is showcased in films like "Indiana Jones and the Last Crusade."

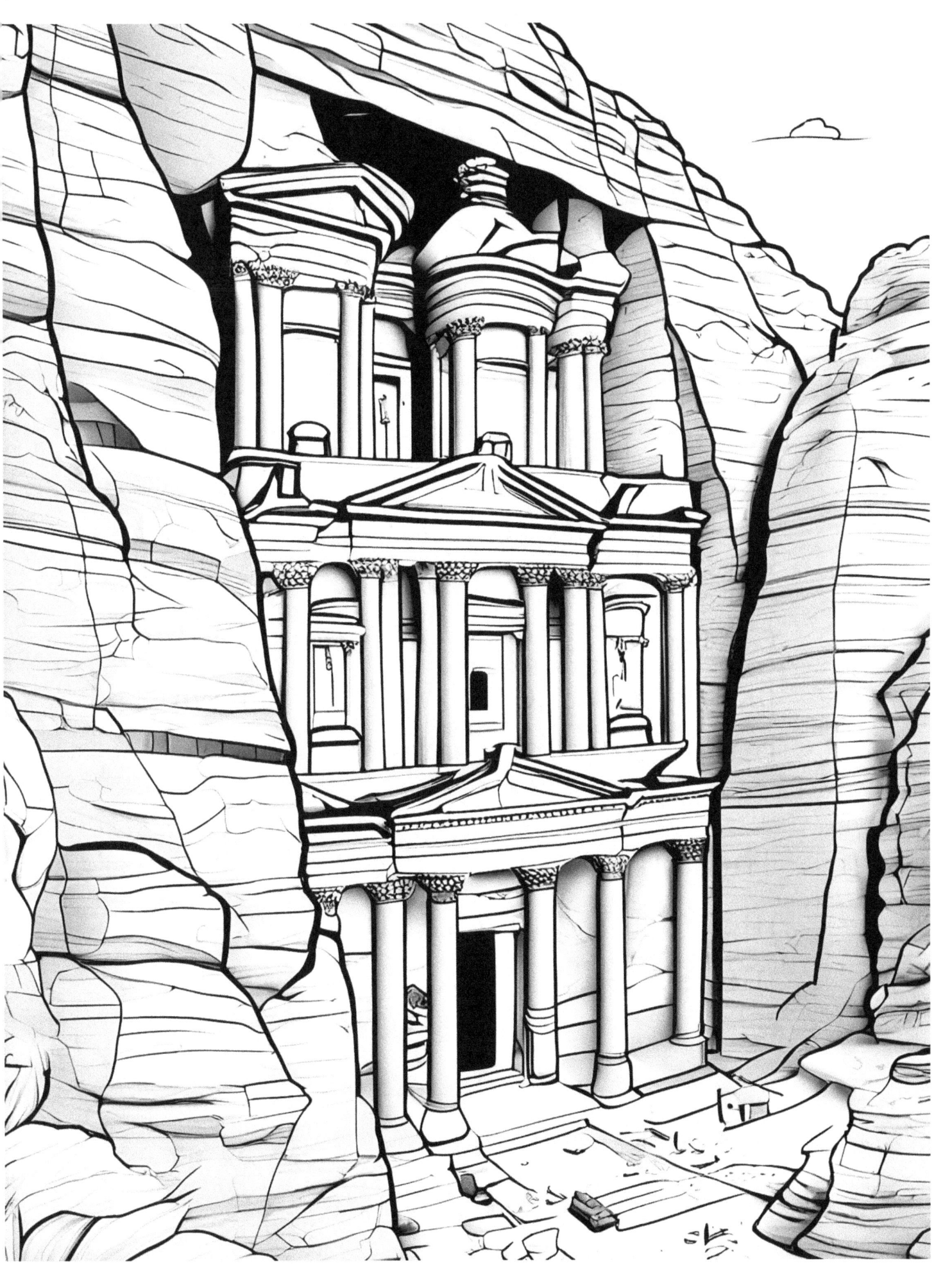

Christ the Redeemer: A Big Statue with Open Arms in Brazil

In Brazil, in a city called Rio de Janeiro, there's a really big statue called Christ the Redeemer. It's like a giant Jesus with arms wide open, welcoming everyone.

The statue is on top of a tall mountain, and it's super huge – 30 meters tall!

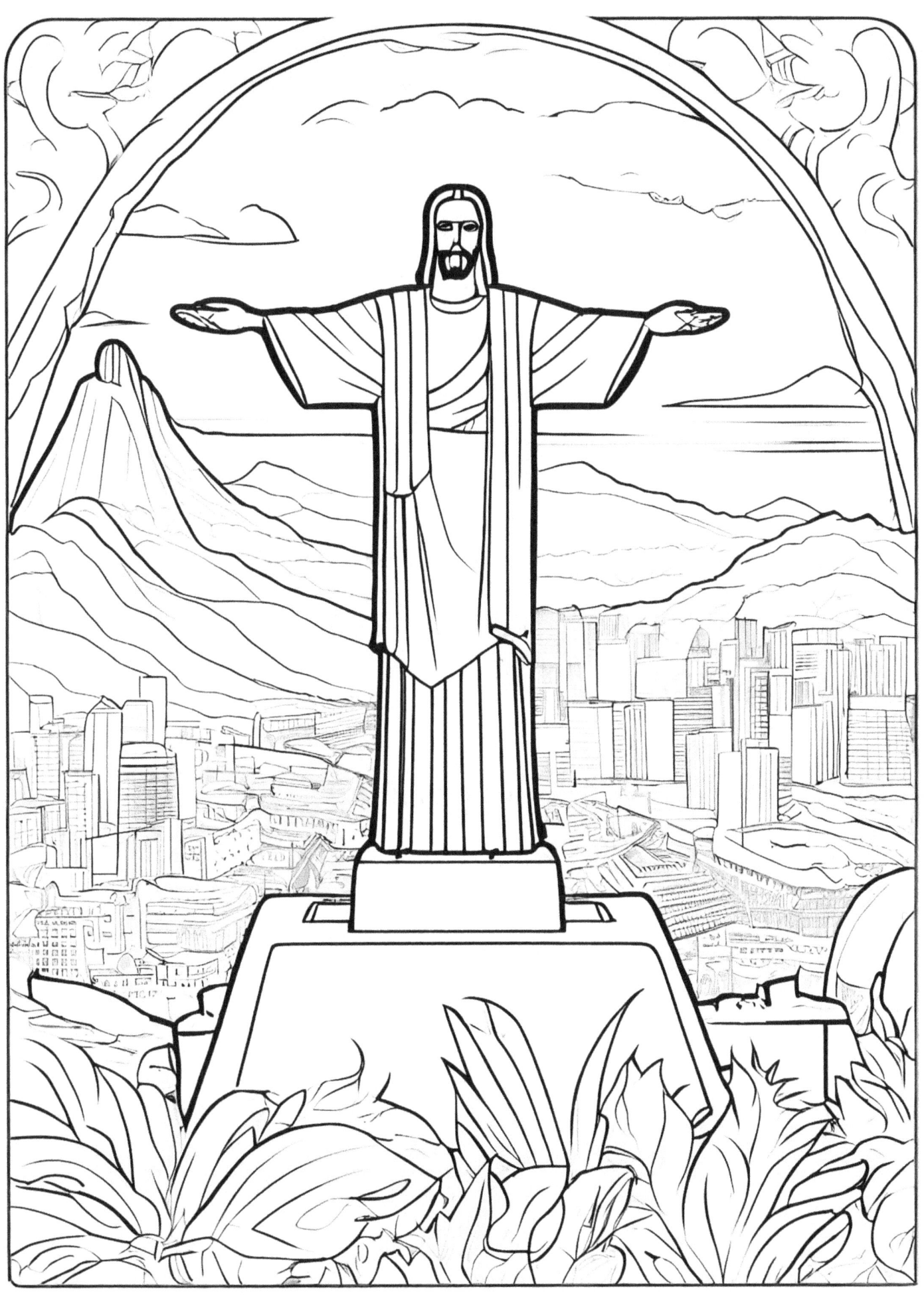

People love going up there to see the amazing views of Rio.

Christ the Redeemer is not just a statue; it's a symbol of welcome and something important for people who follow the Christian religion.

It's like a big friendly greeting to everyone in Rio.

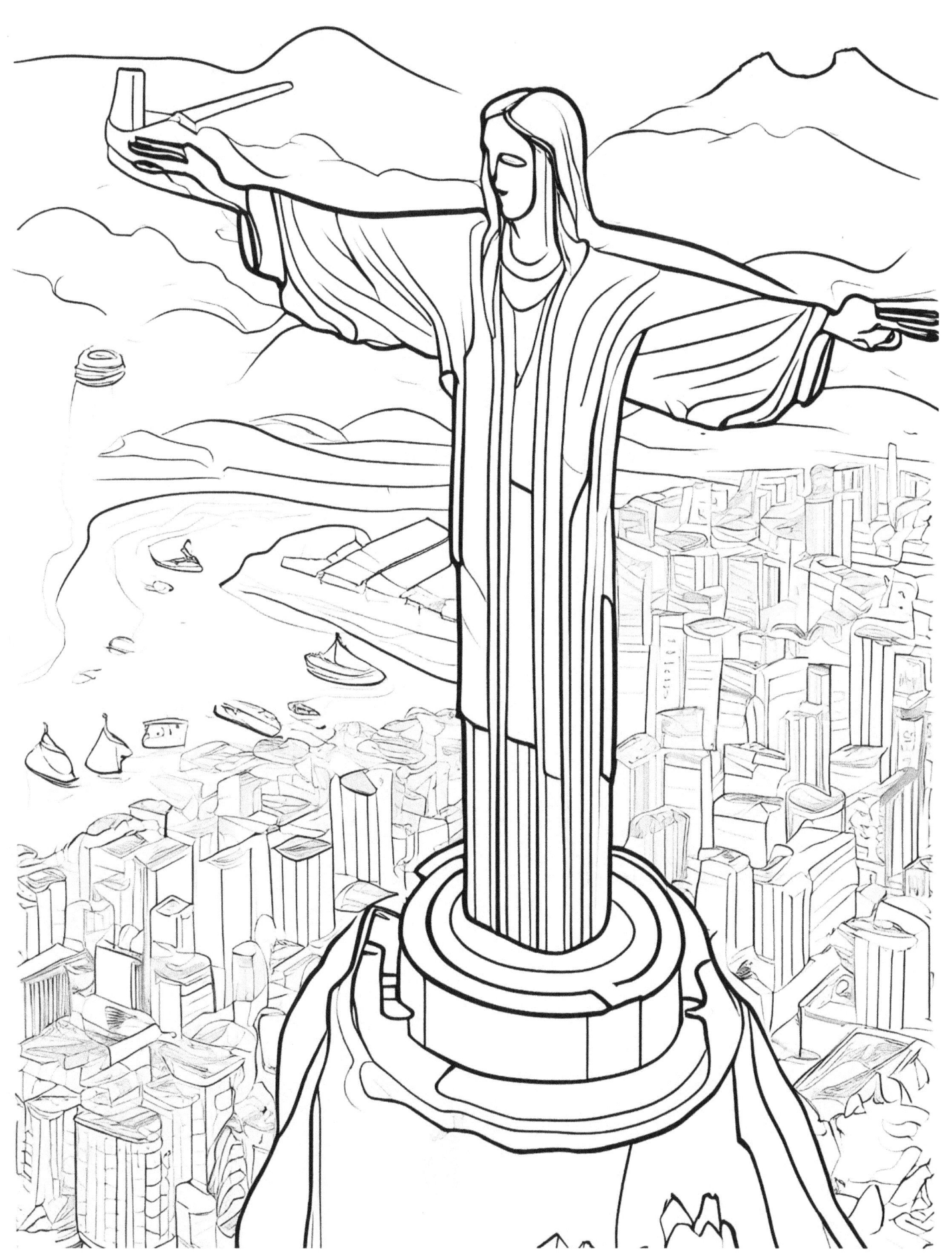

Completed in 1931, Christ the Redeemer was designed by Heitor da Silva Costa and sculpted by Paul Landowski.

Interesting fact: The statue has occasionally been used for events, like being lit up in the colors of various national flags.

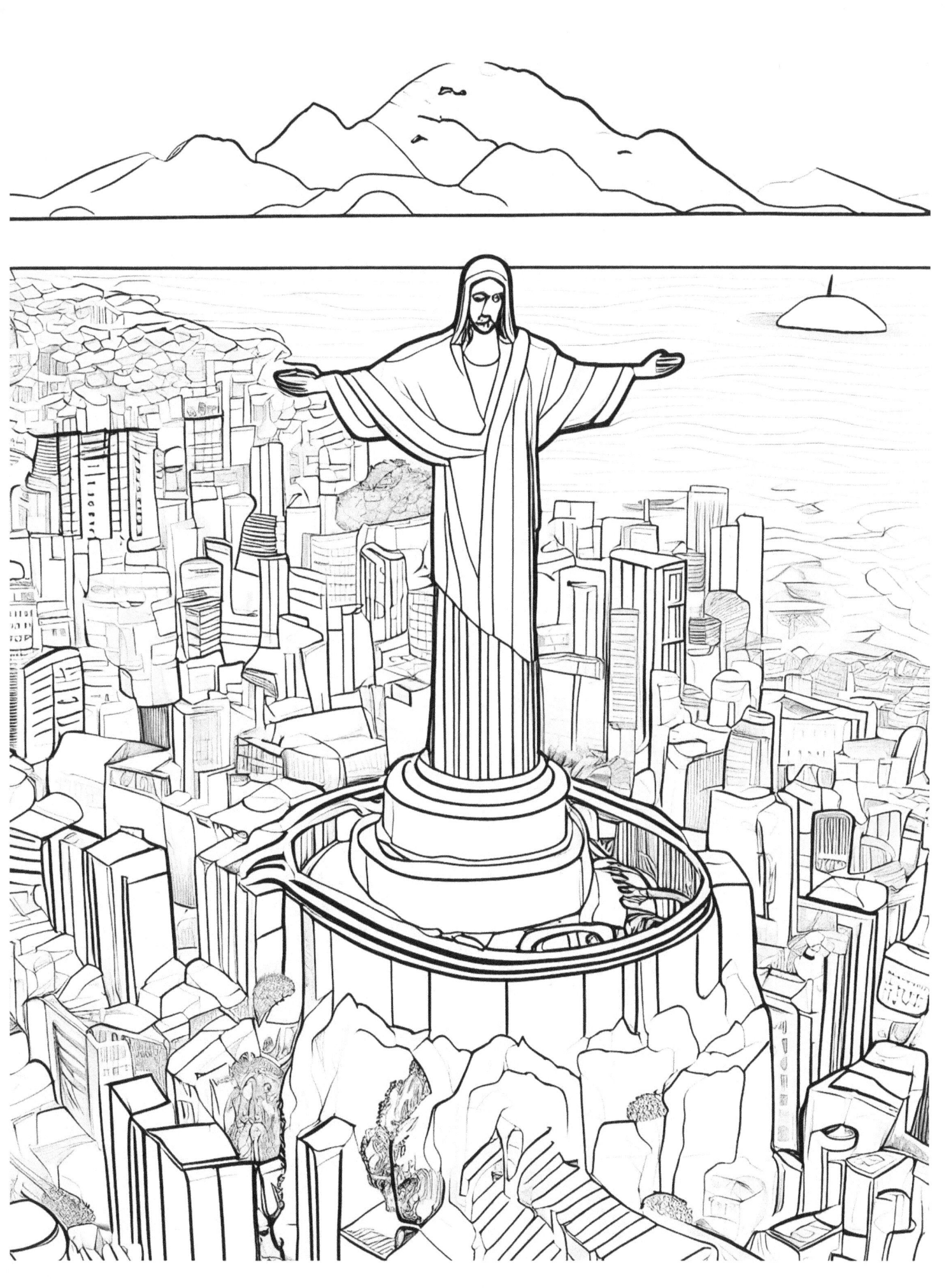

Machu Picchu: an ancient city in the mountains of Peru

In Peru, high in the mountains, there is an ancient city called Machu Picchu.

It's like a hidden treasure because it was forgotten for so long.

The Incas, who were very clever, built it with stones and it has an incredible view.

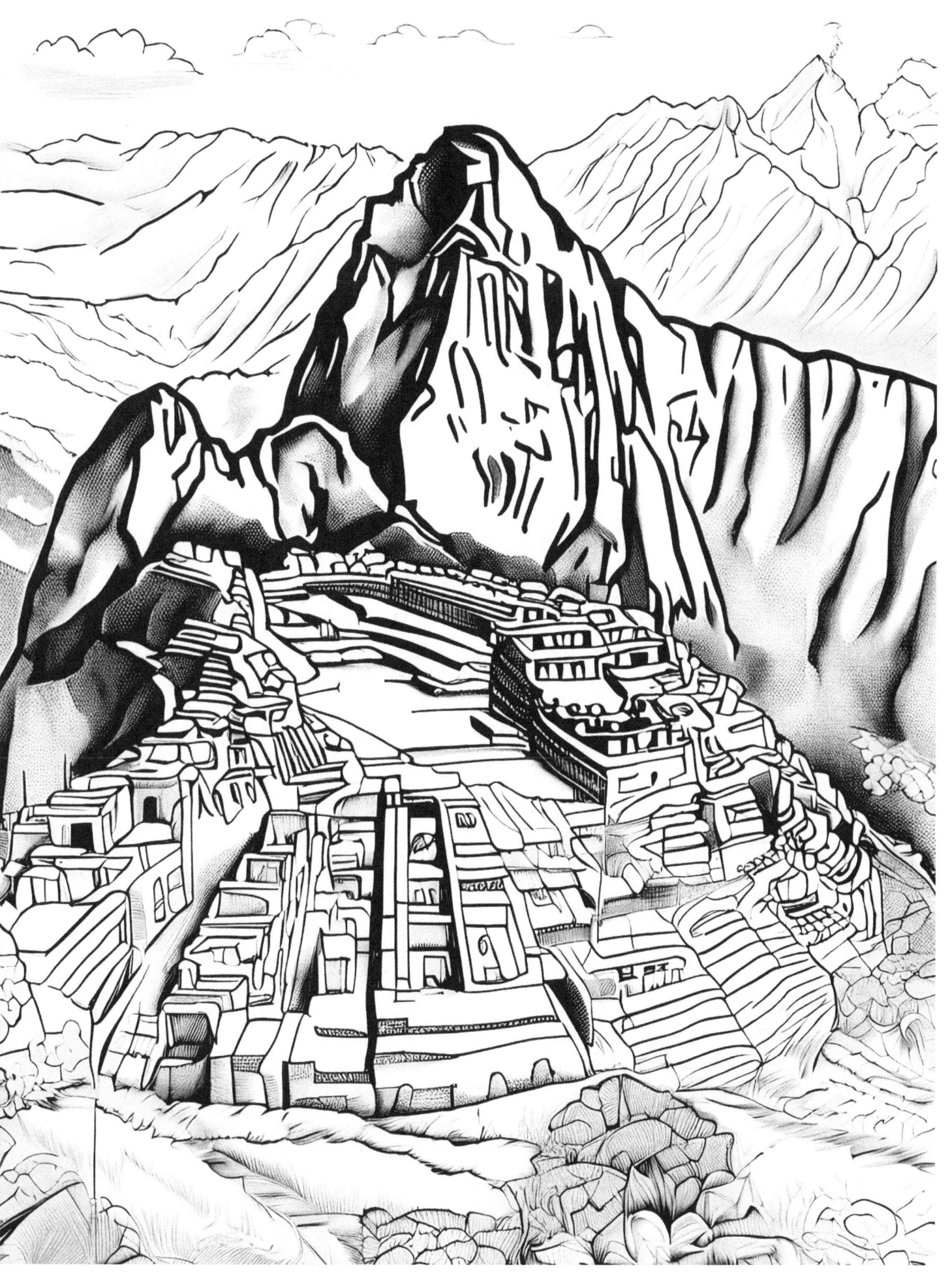

You can see temples, houses and even a special stone called Intihuatana.

People visit Machu Picchu to see the ancient world in the clouds, discovering the mysteries of a city that was lost and found again.

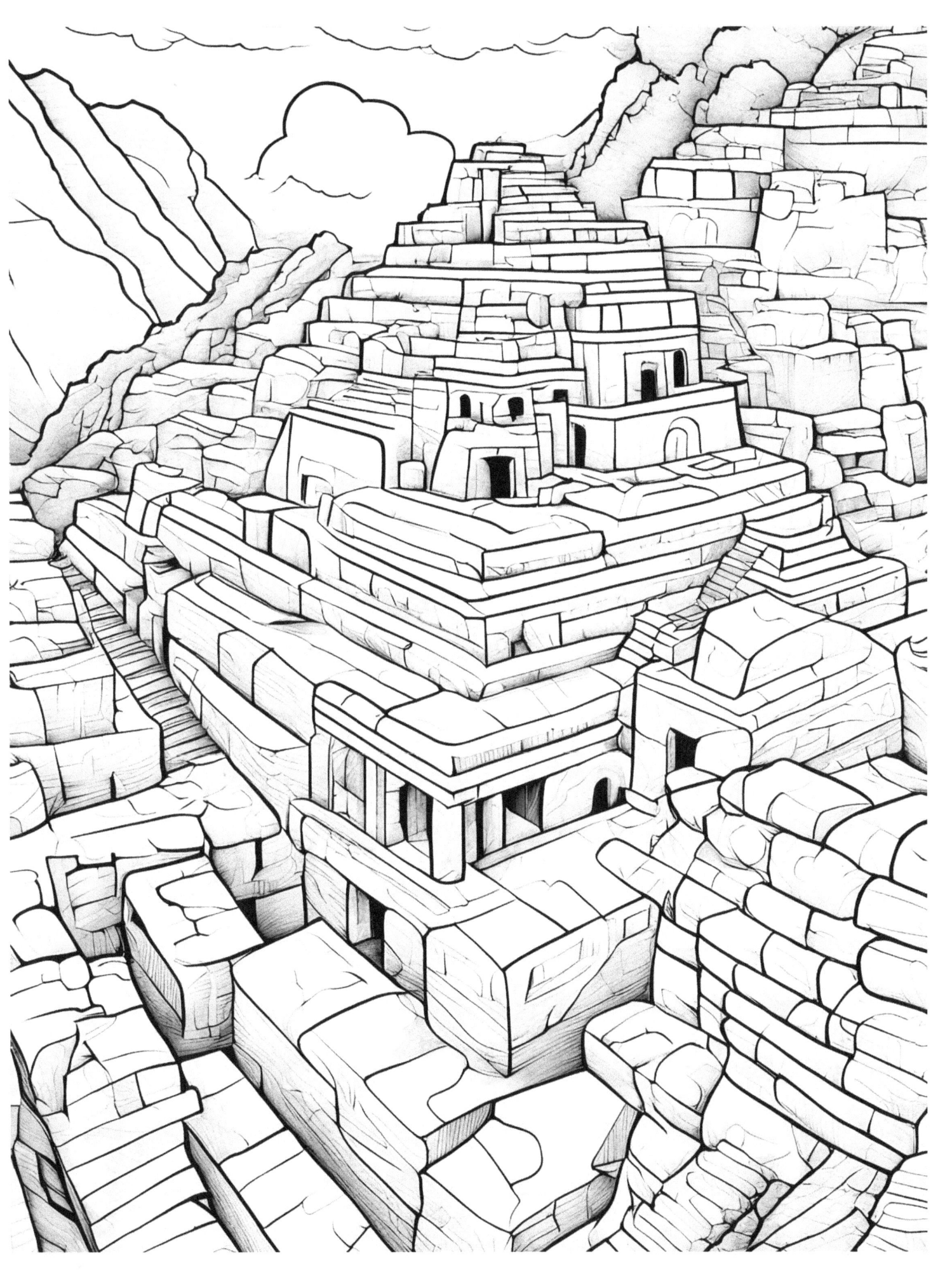

Machu Picchu was built around 1450 AD by Inca Emperor Pachacuti and remained hidden until 1911.

Fun Fact: The Incas were skilled astronomers and Machu Picchu's structures align with astronomical events.

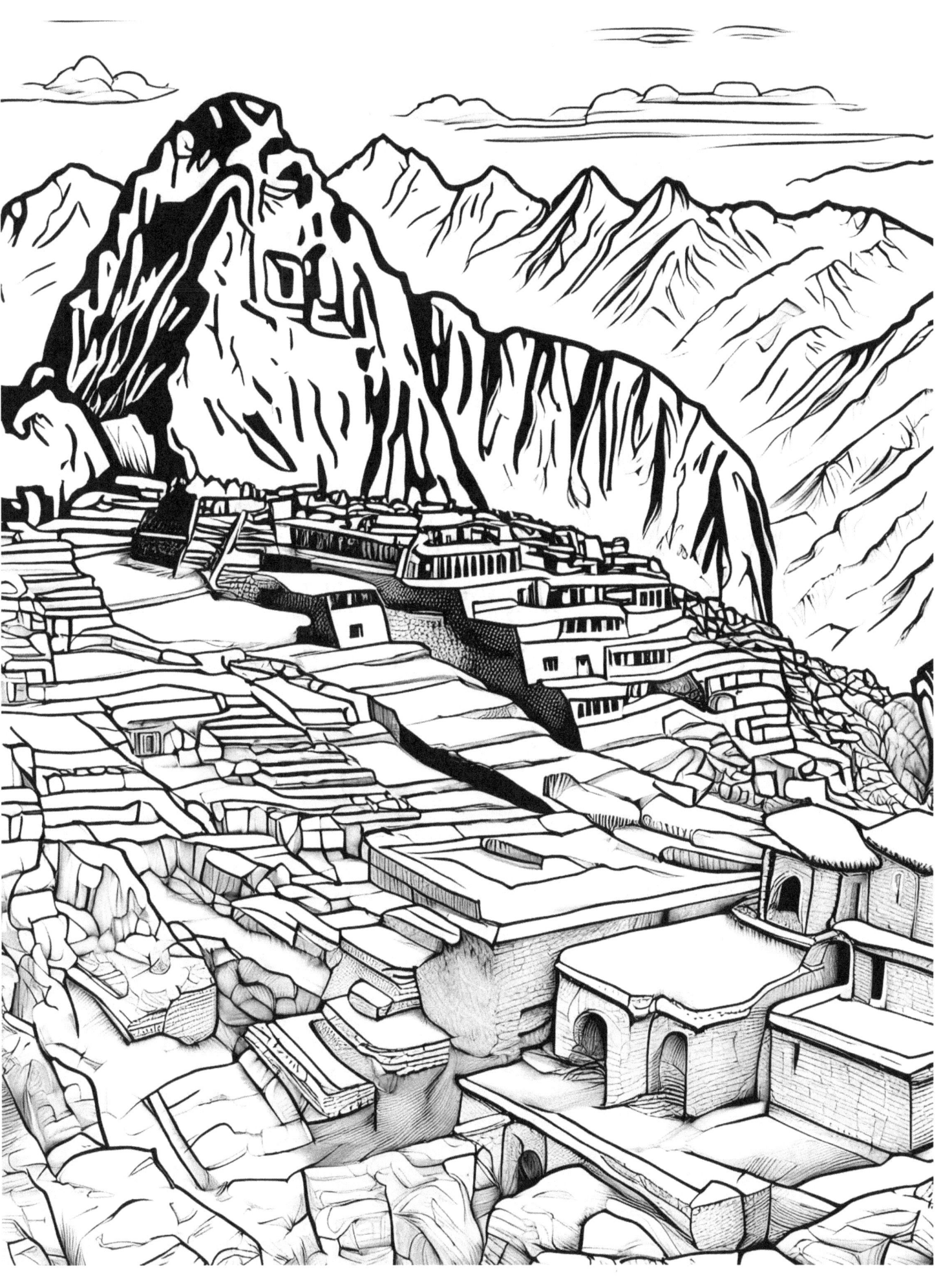

Chichen Itza: Amazing Ruins in Mexico with a Calendar Pyramid

In Mexico, there's a fantastic place with old ruins called Chichen Itza. There's a big pyramid called El Castillo, and it looks like a calendar.

The Mayans, who lived there, did cool ceremonies in a special sinkhole called Cenote Sagrado.

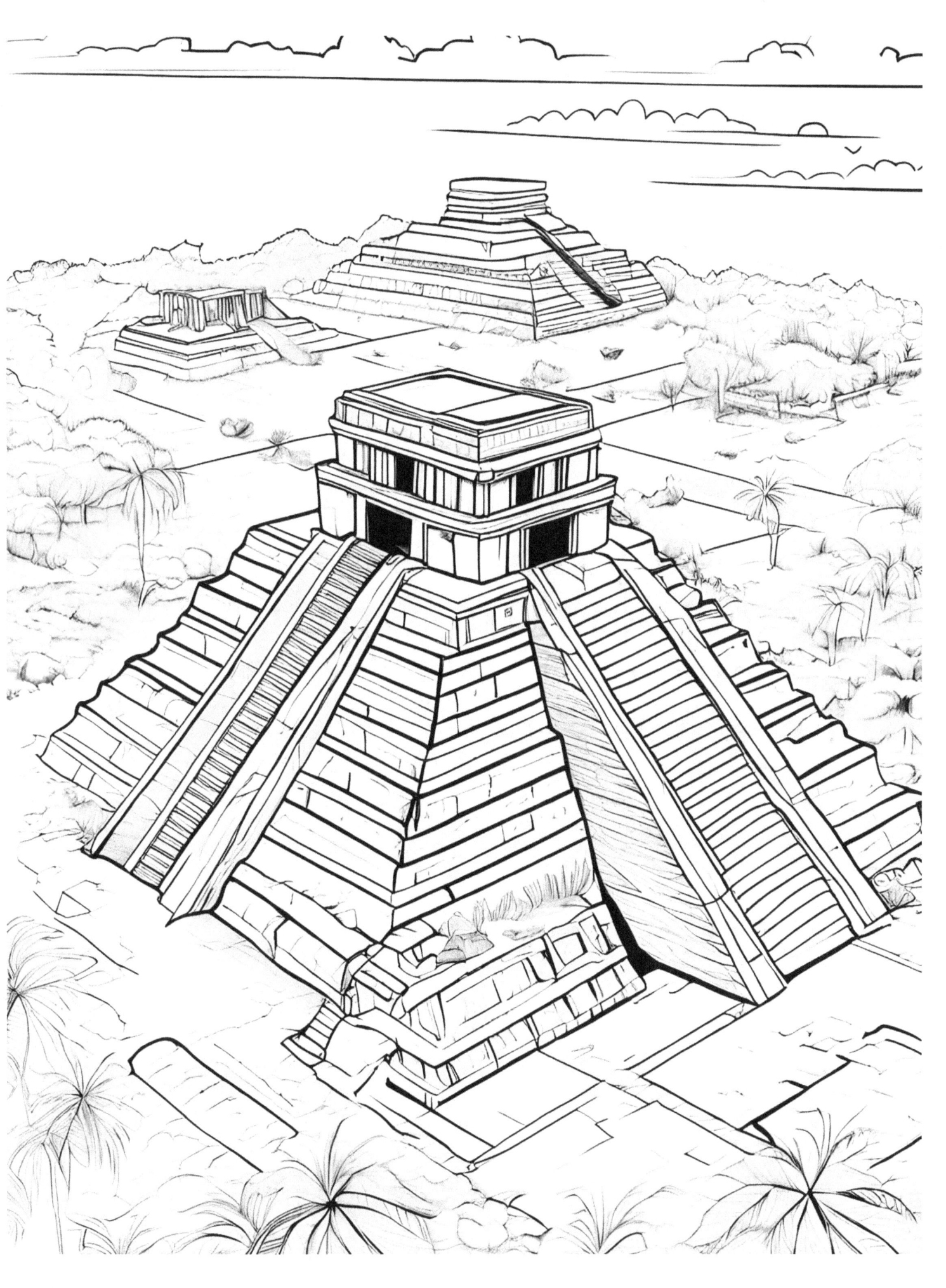

Exploring Chichen Itza is like a trip back in time, discovering the mysteries of an ancient civilization and imagining the people who lived in this amazing place.

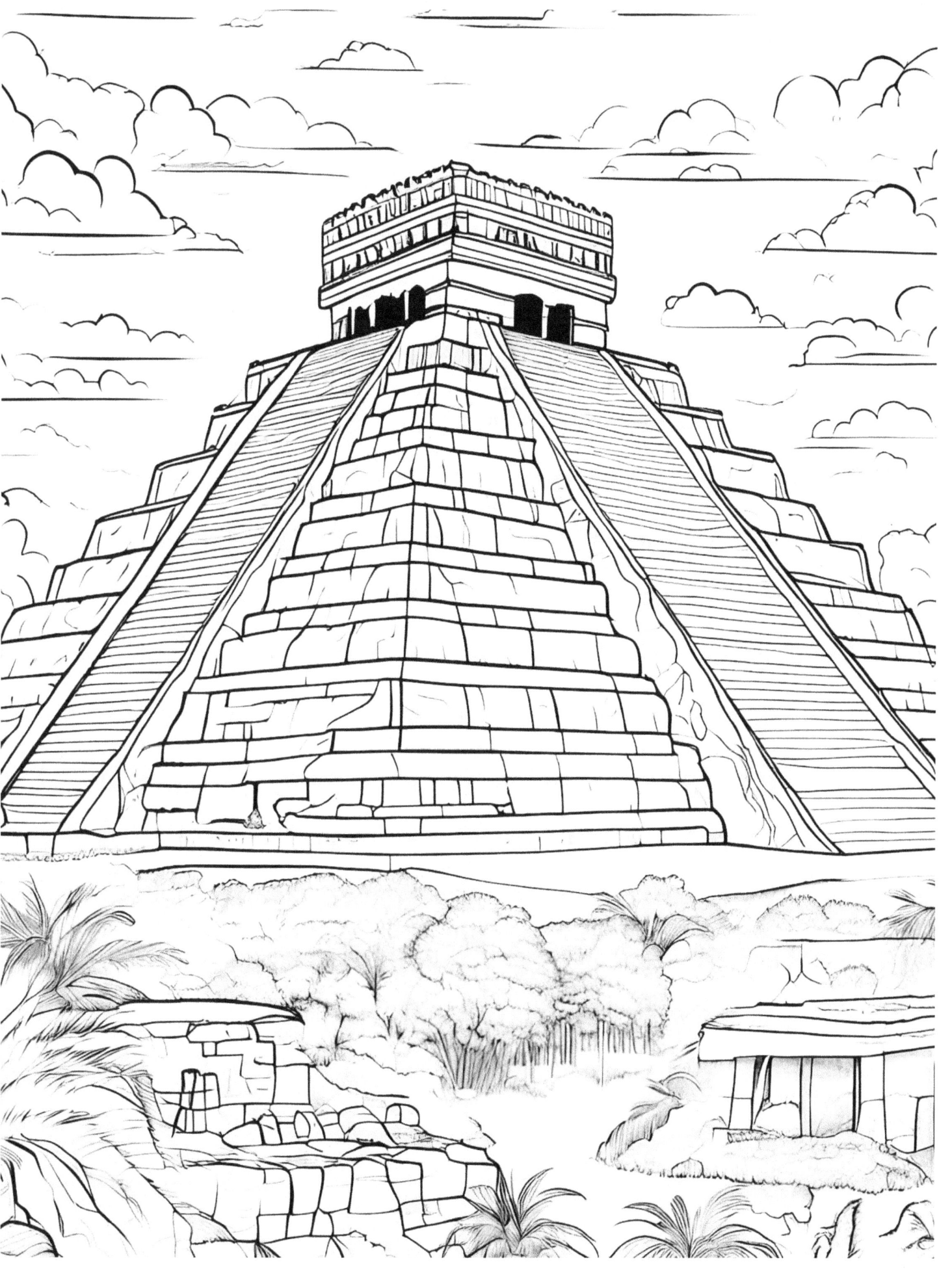

Constructed by the Maya civilization, Chichen Itza thrived from the 6th to 10th century AD. The Pyramid of Kukulkan is a highlight.

Fun fact: Shadows on the pyramid during equinoxes create the illusion of a serpent descending the steps.

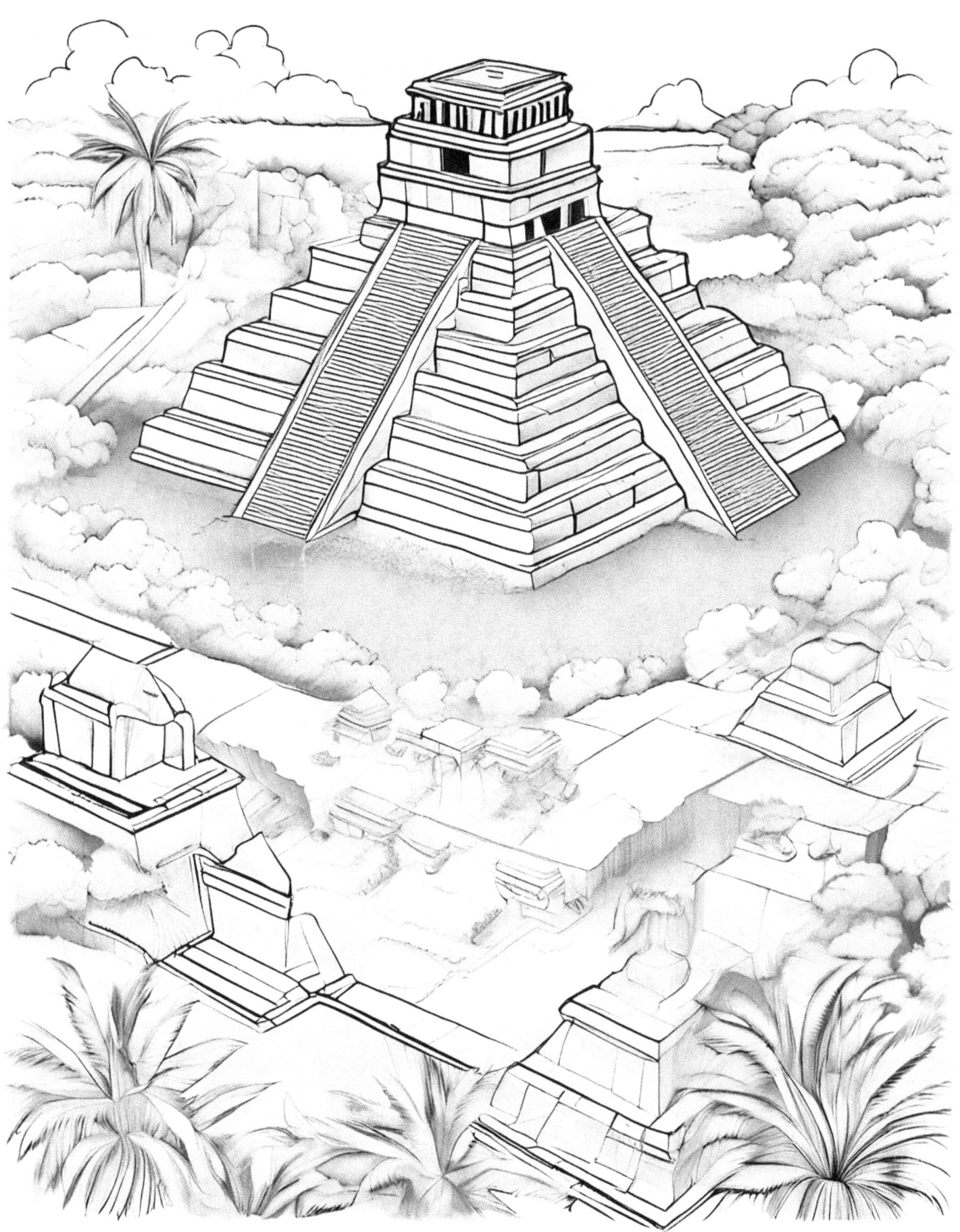

Roman Colosseum: A Huge Arena in Rome for Exciting Shows

In Rome, Italy, there's a gigantic arena called the Roman Colosseum.

It's really old and was used for exciting shows like gladiator fights and animal hunts.

The builders were really smart, and the Colosseum can fit a lot of people.

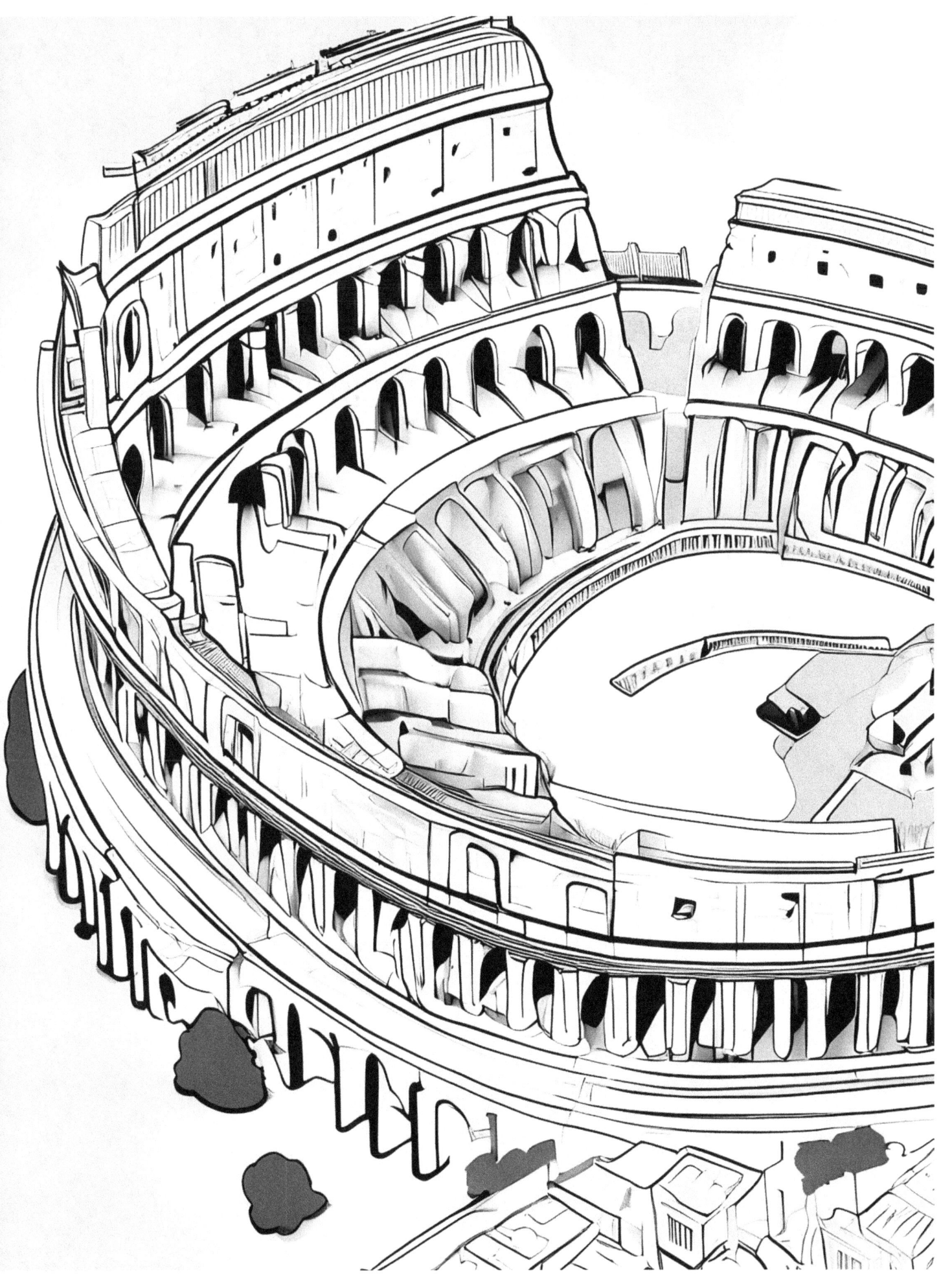

Now, it's like a big history lesson where you can imagine the cheers and roars from the ancient crowds.

The Colosseum is not just an old building; it's a place that takes you back in time to the thrilling events that happened in this huge arena.

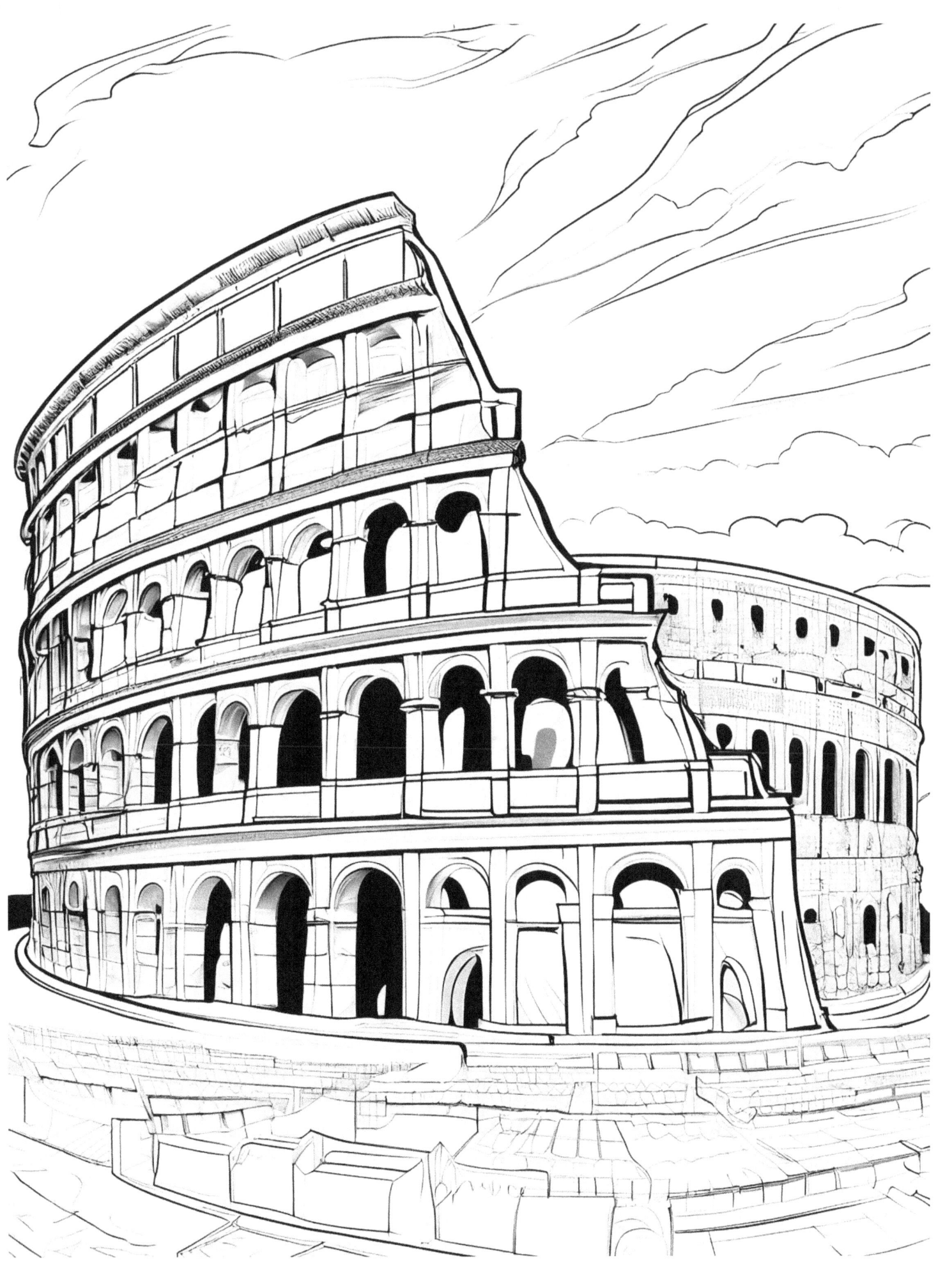

Inaugurated in AD 80, the Colosseum hosted gladiator contests and events. Funded by the spoils of the Jewish War.

Curiosity: The Colosseum could be flooded to host naval battles, thanks to an intricate system of channels.

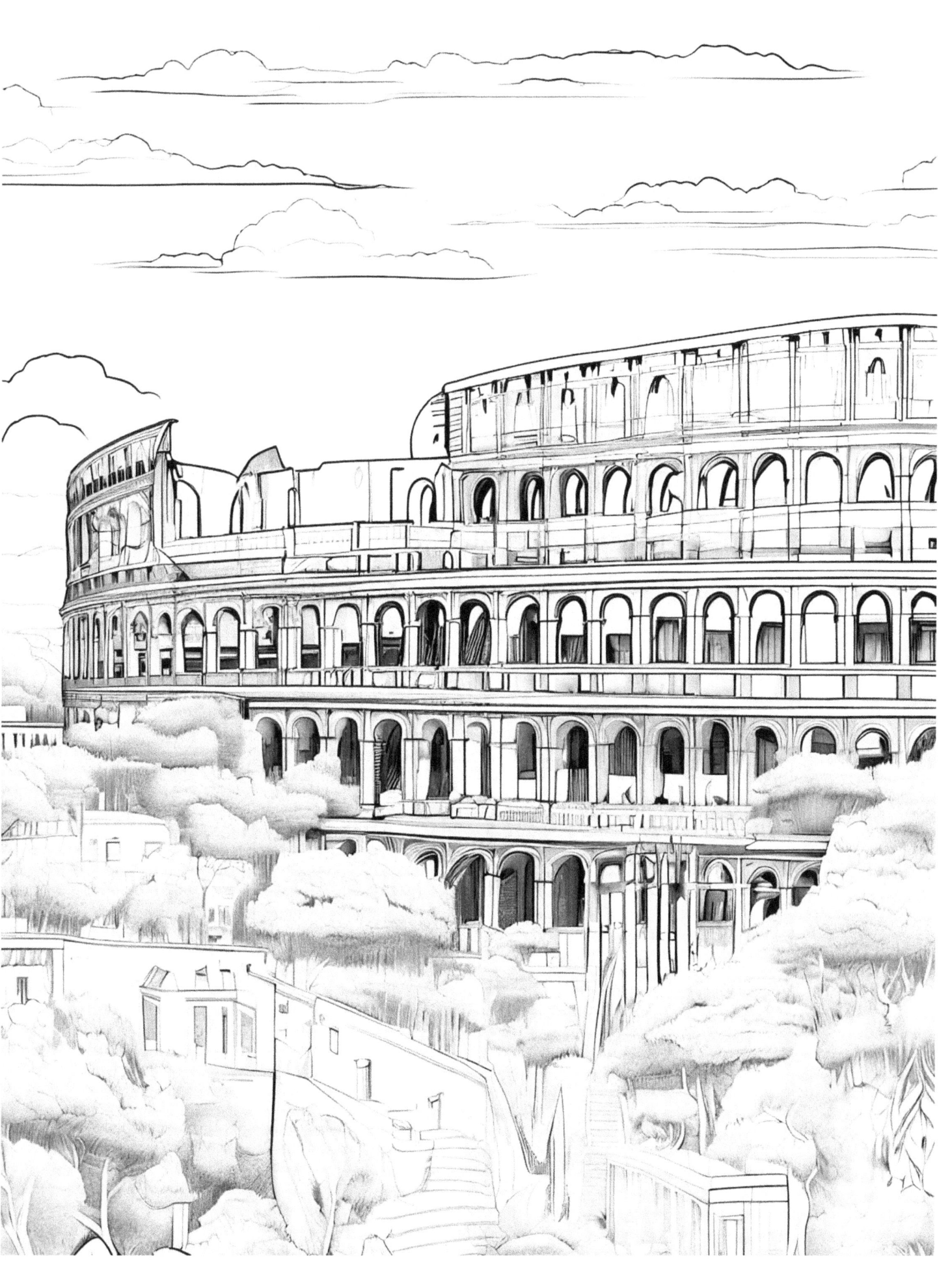

Taj Mahal: A Beautiful Palace in India Built with Love

In India, there's a stunning palace called the Taj Mahal. It's made of white marble and looks like a fairy tale.

It was built a long time ago by an emperor for his beloved wife. The gardens around it are lovely, and the whole place is a symbol of eternal love.

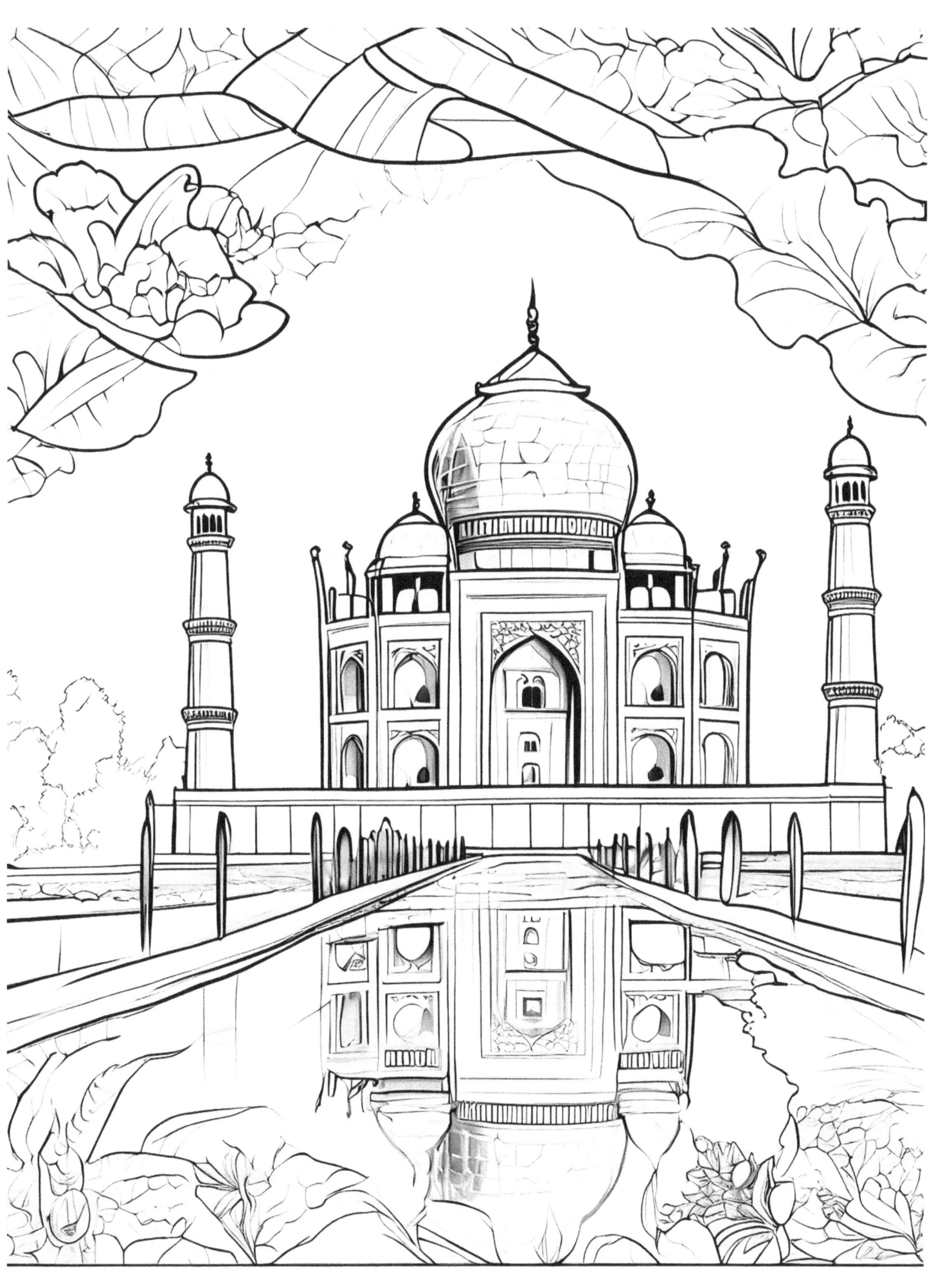

People come to marvel at its beauty and feel the romantic vibes.

The Taj Mahal is not just a palace; it's a place that tells a story of love and craftsmanship, inviting everyone to appreciate its timeless elegance.

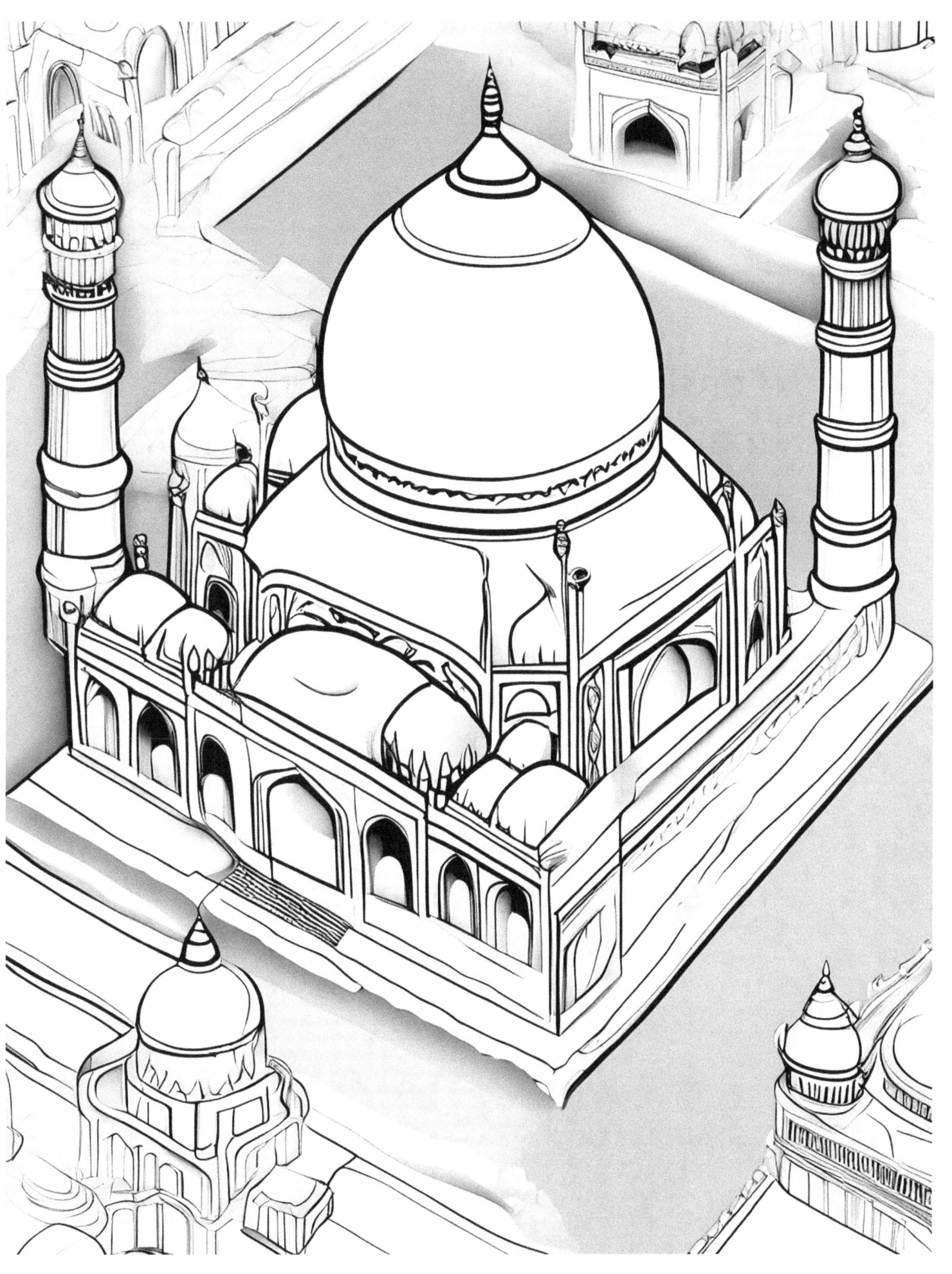

Constructed from 1632 to 1653, the Taj Mahal is a testament to Shah Jahan's love for his wife Mumtaz Mahal.

Interesting fact: The white marble changes color throughout the day, reflecting different moods.

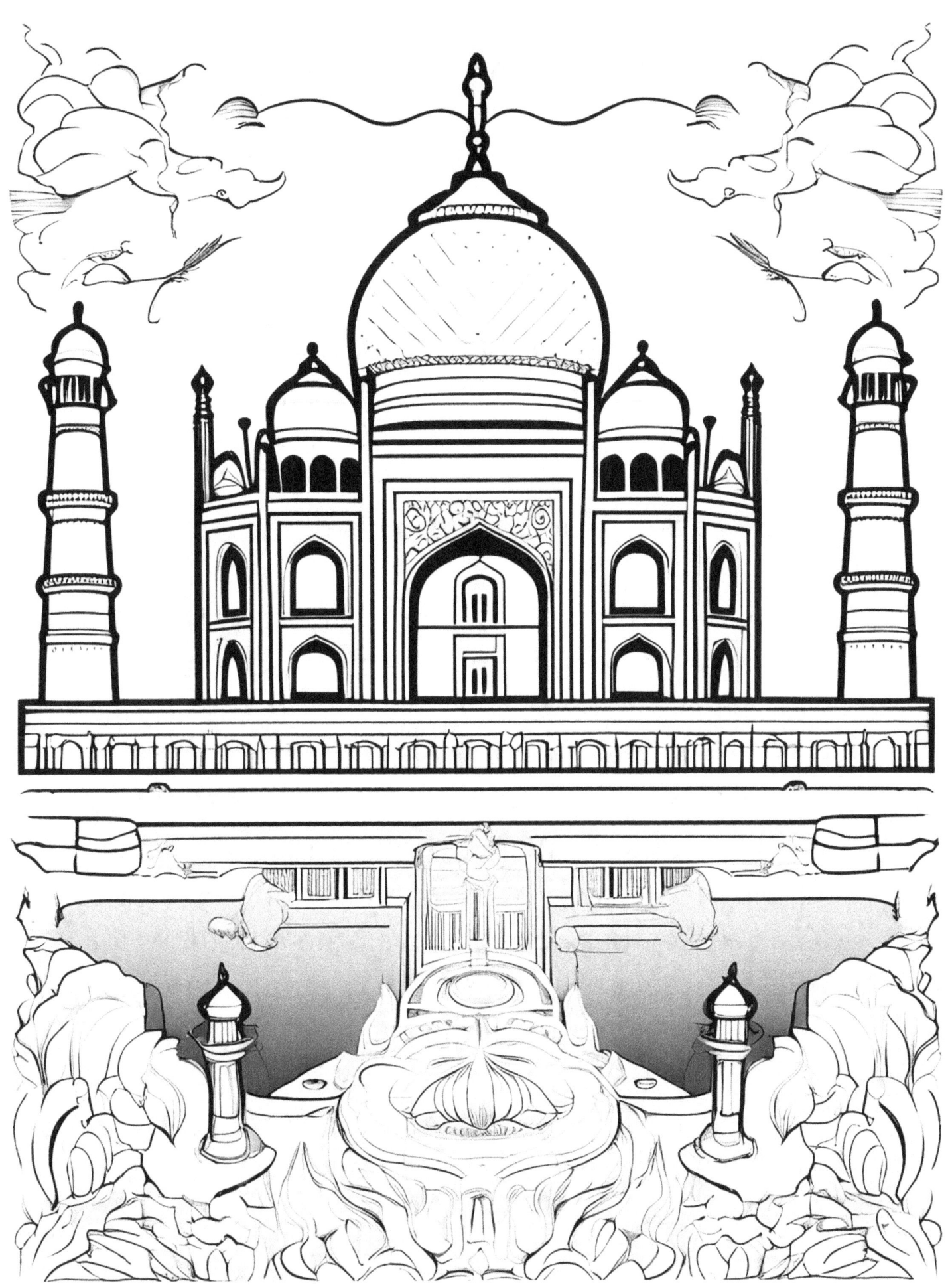

Conclusion and Next Adventure:

As we conclude this colorful odyssey through the modern wonders, we hope "Colors of Wonder" has ignited your creativity and deepened your appreciation for the architectural splendors that grace our world. Your artistic journey through the Great Wall of China, Petra, Christ the Redeemer, Machu Picchu, Chichen Itza, the Roman Colosseum, and the Taj Mahal has been a celebration of both art and history.

As you close this chapter, we extend an invitation to embark on the next adventure in our series – "Colors of Wonder: Timeless Echoes – Coloring the Seven Wonders of the Ancient World". Join us in exploring the Seven Wonders of the Ancient World, from the magnificent Pyramid of Giza to the enchanting Hanging Gardens of Babylon. Uncover the mysteries of these timeless wonders and continue your artistic voyage through the ages.

Thank you for being part of our colorful journey. Until we meet again in the pages of ancient marvels, happy coloring!